The Human Character

Self help

The Human Character

Abdenal Carvalho

SUMMARY

Preface 9

First Part 11

    The Human Personality 13

    The human character of Christ 16

    The Moral Character of Christ... 19

    The Divine Character of Christ.. 22

    The Human Emotional Character 26

    What is Solitude?... 28

    How to Avoid Loneliness? 28

    How does depression develop?.. 30

    A Brief Concept of Happiness... 33

    Concepts About Love... 38

Love is an Antidote Against Loneliness 40

How to Practice Love? 42

More About God's Pure Love 45

Faith Awakens God's Love for His Children 46

How to Be Happy Despite Afflictions? 49

We are what we think 50

Be Someone Enlightened 51

Personality Flaws 53

The Fruits of Human Meat 58

How to Be Socially Accepted 62

Segunda Parte 65

Reflections: Psalm 119: 100 67

Reflections: Isaiah 53: 4 69

Reflections: II Corinthians 12: 9 71

Reflections: Romans 9: 28 73

Reflections: Matthew 16: 13-15 75

Reflection: Jonah 3: 5.. 77

Reflections: Genesis 11: 6 79

Reflection: Colossians 2: 13-14 81

Reflection: James 4: 7 83

Reflexão: Salmos 23: 4 85

Reflection: Psalm 23: 4 87

Reflection: Matthew 5: 44 89

Human Egoism 91

The Character of the Modern Christian....................................... 98

Corruption of Human Gender 100

As Características Morais da Verdadeira Igreja 102

The Character of Man as a Creature 104

The Character of Man as the Son of God................................... 105

Considerações Finais...

Bibliografia...

Preface

All of us, human beings, were created and endowed with the ability to relate to each other in an emotional, rational and intellectual way that makes them different from other living beings on this planet, forming groups of individuals according to race, color, religious creed and politically organized.

Thus, it is extremely necessary that we have permanent contact with each other so that there is a harmonious and social coexistence, avoiding the state of loneliness that is the biggest cause of serious psychological illnesses that lead many to a psychiatric condition that is often irreversible.

"The Human Character" is another work created with the objective of contributing to the logical reasoning of our readers about the importance of daily contact with our peers, whether they are friends, family, neighbors or even with the strangers that we encounter in the course of the day the day. I hope it is being useful to everyone as they honor us with reading each article published in this book and that the advice and guidelines mentioned here contribute to the well-being of each individual.

First Part

The Human Personality

The human being was created with the ability to adapt to the environment in which he lives, however, each person in particular has his own personality that differentiates him from the others. In this way we can find in a single social group different types of thoughts, ideas, concepts and reasoning about certain subjects. This is because each individual interprets life, the world, its own existence and terms, such as: Religion, politics, science, past, present and future with its individual perspective.

And this is something very useful because what would become of humanity if everyone acted and thought the same way? This diversity of mentalities, one opposing the other, has allowed man to reach the highest point of his discoveries.

Today we fly and cross the limits of outer space with airplanes and ships that allow us to know the Universe that was previously misunderstood. We travel in gigantic ships or submerged in powerful submarines. Man, through his perspicacity and tenacity, built powerful weapons of war to defeat his enemies, science alongside medicine discovered the cure for epidemics that soon spread over the land, culminating in the deaths of millions of people.

All this scientific, cultural, social, religious and political evolution has only happened because humanity is not homogeneous, that is, we are different from each other and have opposite ideas from each other. While some believe in the impossible, others believe that they can touch the stars and walk on them. The human personality is divided into four groups, namely:

1. Physical Character

2. Psychological character

3. Moral character

4. Spiritual character

1. Physical Character — It is directly linked to our physical appearance, our body with its individual and unique characteristics. There are beautiful, attractive and desirous people, however there are also those who have been prevented from such virtue.

Each one carries in his luggage that good or bad inherited in his own human nature, however this type of character does not diminish in the individual the possibility of him having other attributes that surpass his little external beauty. There are those who hate the mirror not to see its disgusting appearance, but it is highly intelligent and endowed with many gifts.

There are others who, despite their extreme physical beauty, have an IQ so low that hearing what they say in their dialogues is repulsive. Therefore, we understand that physical character is not the most essential part of human personality.

2. Psychological Character — Defines the way we think, act, relate to other people, face life and its surprises, the way we overcome each obstacle that appears during our walk in this world, our inner strength or weakness. People whose psychological status is weak tend to be afraid to face life, live fully and choose anonymity.

3. Moral Character — As the concept itself makes clear, this is the extreme point between modesty and its absence in interpersonal relationships in the social environment. Individuals without a minimum of morality do not respect, honor their fellow men, nor are they fulfilling their commitments with dignity. Furthermore, they are immoral and refuse to believe and follow those who trust in God. The moral character reveals who we really are and which side we belong to, whether in light or in darkness.

4. Spiritual Character — This is the side of man's relationship with his Creator, the human soul and spirit.

Here are kept your faith, your religious beliefs, your spiritual inclination and your ability to understand life after death. And all these aspects form the Human Character.

The human character of Christ

By leaving his kingdom of glory and coming to this world, occupying a form that would allow him to relate physically with the other people of his time so that it would be possible to tell them about the divine plans of salvation, Christ, in the likeness of man , came to have its own personality and a peculiar human character like each one of us has, but without sin. About who Jesus was, detailing his physical and personal characteristics, the prophet Isaiah quoted, in his book, centuries before the following description:

"Because it went up as a growth before him, and as the root of a dry land; he had neither beauty nor beauty, and, looking at him, there was no good appearance in him, that we might wish him.

He was despised, and the most rejected among men, a man of pain, and experienced at work; and, as one from whom men hid their faces, he was despised, and we made no case of him. Truly he took our infirmities upon himself, and took our pains upon himself; and we regarded him as afflicted.

Wounded by God, and oppressed. But he was wounded because of our transgressions, and crushed because of our iniquities. The punishment that brings us peace was upon him, and by his stripes we were healed. We were all straying like sheep; each went astray on his way; but the Lord caused the iniquity of us all to fall on him.

He was oppressed and afflicted, but he did not open his mouth; as a lamb was taken to the slaughterhouse, and as the sheep changes before its shearers, so he did not open his mouth.

From oppression and judgment was taken; and who will count the time of your life? Because he was cut off from the land of the living; for the transgression of my people he was hit.

And they laid his grave with the wicked, and with the rich in his death; although he never committed injustice, nor was there any mistake in his mouth.However, the Lord pleased to grind him, making him sick; when his soul sets out to atone for sin, he will see his posterity, he will prolong his days; and the good pleasure of the Lord will prosper in your hand.

He will see the fruit of his soul's work, and be satisfied; with his knowledge my servant, the just, will justify many; because their iniquities will take on you.

"Therefore I will give him the share of many, and with the mighty he will share the spoil; because he poured out his soul in death, and was numbered with transgressors; but he took upon himself the sin of many, and interceded for transgressors." Isaiah 53: 2-12

As we read in the biblical text above, Jesus had a physical appearance common to most men of his time, completely different from that image created by the exceptional painters Leonardo da Vinci and Michelangelo, with the appearance of a European with long blond hair and eyes blue, when in fact Christ was born in Palestine where the sun was continually scorching and its inhabitants had dark skin. The prophet, in describing in his book the vision he received from God about the appearance of the Messiah makes it very clear that he would not be so beautiful as not to cause any admiration in anyone who observed him, as we read:

"Because it went up as a growth before him, and as the root of a dry land; he had neither beauty nor beauty, and, looking at him, there was no good appearance in him, that we might wish him.

He was despised, and the most rejected among men, a man of pain, and experienced at work; and, as one from whom men hid their faces, he was despised, and we made no case of it." Isaiah 53:2

"Soon, his physical character did not cause any admiration in people, but his actions led many to follow him for the miracles that before the perplexed looks he performed continuously." **Isaiah 53:3**

The Moral Character of Christ

Isaiah also cited details about the moral character of Christ when he stated that he himself was willing to come into this world to suffer on a cross in order to "heal our pains and heal our wounds" (v.4), thus revealing his immense love for all of us.

Who would stop living inside a palace, surrounded by people who loved and admired him, adored and respected to suffer the worst humiliations, then be killed crucified on a rude cross just to grant forgiveness and freedom to someone who was imprisoned due to his own crimes and sins consciously practiced and of which he was pleased?

For the Son of God made that important decision and left everything he was and possessed to come to this world to surrender to the hands of his oppressors. In order to allow you and me the possibility of complete reconciliation with your Father. The prophet, stated:

"Truly he took our infirmities upon himself, and took our pains upon himself.

And we regarded him as afflicted, wounded by God, and oppressed. But he was hurt because of our transgressions. It was ground because of our iniquities."

Jesus Christ was morally indisputable, perfect, just, faithful and determined to carry out his redemptive mission to the end. At no time, even in the anguish of death, did he regret coming to our aid.

Of course, like every human being, he feared physical death, even though he was aware of being a God and that death would have no effect on his spirit, however, in the end he surrendered to the Father's will and carried out his mission, as we read in the following text:

"And going a little farther, he fell on his face, praying and saying, My Father, if it is possible, pass this cup from me; however, not as I want, but as you want. " **Matthew 26:39**

For a second he seems to want to retreat, that was the norm because he was in the shape of a man, it was his humanity that reacted that way. But soon after, he surrenders to the will of his Father, who has filled him with grace and power, giving them strength and courage to continue until the end. This makes us realize something exceptional about our relationship with God. When, for some reason.

We are tempted to give up our struggles and conquests we must look only to the Lord, through faith, and we will be empowered to move forward, overcoming all obstacles.

Another strong point in Christ's moral character was his incomparable ability to forgive his enemies even at the most extreme point of his martyrdom. There, nailed to the cross, dying little by little while the Roman soldiers shared their clothes and cast lots among themselves, their veins emptied of the blood that would purify everyone from that day onwards to believe in him, he still had the strength to ask the Father to tell them forgive:

"And Jesus said: Father, forgive them, because they do not know what they are doing. And, dividing their clothes, they cast lots." **Luke 23:34**

No other human being would have such humility, only Jesus was able to forgive his opponents to death. This characteristic shows how faithful our Lord is and his infinite love for us. His earthly ministry lasted for about three years and he lived in Palestine for thirty-three years, as the scriptures claim, but he never committed any sin. As the author of the letter to the Hebrews made clear:

"Because we do not have a high priest who cannot sympathize with our weaknesses; but one who, like us, was tempted in everything, but without sin." **Hebrews 4:15**

Therefore, Jesus Christ was a perfect man in all his ways, without any spot or stain of transgressions, which makes him unique. His trajectory in this world did not cause scandals that today anyone can point out and blame him for some error or sin, his enemies could accuse him of several other things, such as blasphemy for having declared himself the Messiah, the Only Begotten Son of God, the Savior of the lost, but never for having committed any kind of iniquity.

The Divine Character of Christ

In occupying the human form, the Son of God lost all his powers as a God and became a little less than the angels, as the writer says to the Hebrews:

"You made it a little smaller than the angels. You crowned him with glory and honor and made him over the works of your hands." Hebrews 2: 7

In this biblical quotation we understand two very important things: First that in taking up the human form the Messiah lost his power as God. And, second, that he needed to be clothed with the power of the Holy Spirit in order to be able to work miracles, because if the Father he placed in a position inferior to angels such things would not be possible among men.Since angels do not work wonders on earth.

Although many modern sects affirm the opposite of what the Scriptures teach. In this way, Jesus had to go to meet John, at the Jordan River, to be baptized in water. First to serve as an example to all future Christians, as there is no complete salvation of the soul without the complete remission of ancient sins, through water baptism, as we read in the Holy Scriptures in this regard:

"Whoever believes and is baptized will be saved; but whoever does not believe will be condemned." **Mark 16:16**

Right after the water baptism, Christ was invested one hundred percent of the power of the Holy Spirit so that he could begin his ministry in a glorious way and have the courage to endure all the martyrdom he experienced during the three years he preached the Good News of Salvation to Satan's captives.

We need to understand something quite complex on this particular subject: In reality, even though he was a God in the form of a man, it was not Jesus, in himself, who worked the miracles and wonders witnessed by hundreds of Palestinians more than two thousand years ago, but the Holy Spirit who landed on him on the day of baptism, just as it is today in the heart of the church. No Christian who has not yet received the Anointing of the Spirit has gifts of healing, prophecies, revelations, or anything else. For God cannot work through him without first being baptized with water and fire.

John himself taught this to his disciples even before Christ came to meet him.

"John answered them all, saying, I, indeed, baptize you with water, but, behold, he who is more powerful than me, from whom I am not worthy to untie the strap of sandals. He will baptize you with the Holy Spirit and fire." Luke 3:16

Therefore, we can understand that throughout his earthly ministry, the miracle worker was the Holy Spirit God and not the Christ. For this reason he warned his listeners to be zealous not to blaspheme against the Spirit, since it is the only sin without possibilities of forgiveness, as we read:

"Therefore, I say to you, All sin and blasphemy will be forgiven men; but blasphemy against the Spirit will not be forgiven men." Matthew 12:31

Christ's divine character has all the same attributes as God the Father and God the Holy Spirit. He is also eternal, infinite, all powerful, omniscient, omnipresent, omnipotent. He knows all things, is present everywhere, has unlimited power and reigns over the heavens and the earth. Without a doubt, Jesus was the Messiah incarnated in the form of a man. Who suffered an undeserved and cruel martyrdom for the love of all of us. And he himself will return to this world, not to atone for sins again.

But to separate his sheep from the goats, the faithful from the infidels, and give to each according to his works, defeating Satan and then casting him into the lake of fire together with his fallen angels, accompanied by those who rejected salvation. The day of his coming will be glorious and is awaited by all those who love him with immense anxiety, but unbelievers will be a day of fear.

"Woe to those who desire the Lord's day! What do you want this day of the Lord for? It will be darkness and not light." Amos 5:18

"Is not the day of the Lord, then, darkness, not light, and darkness, without brightness?" Amos 5:20

"And I saw an angel coming down from heaven, who had the key to the abyss, and a great chain in his hand. He trapped the dragon, the ancient serpent, which is the Devil and Satan, and tied him up for a thousand years. And he threw him into the abyss.

And closed him there, and put a seal on him, lest he deceive the nations again, until the thousand years are ended. And then it matters that he be released for a little while. And I saw thrones; and they sat on them, and they were given the power to judge. And I saw the souls of those who were beheaded by the testimony of Jesus.

And by the word of God, and who did not worship the beast or his image, and did not receive the mark on their foreheads or in their hands; and lived, and reigned with Christ for a thousand years.

But the other dead did not live again, until the thousand years were over. This is the first resurrection. Blessed and holy is he who has a part in the first resurrection; the second death has no power over these; but they will be priests of God and of Christ, and will reign with him a thousand years.

And he said to me more: It is fulfilled. I am Alpha and Omega, the beginning and the end. To whoever is thirsty, I will give it free of charge from the source of the water of life.

Whoever wins will inherit all things; and I will be your God, and he will be my son." Revelation 21: 1-7

The Human Emotional Character

Our emotions are directly linked to the feelings of the soul, that is, the human body is concerned with showing externally what our inner being feels before each phase of life, in good and bad times, whether joys or sadnesses and this is called the our Emotional Character. There are the strongest that almost nothing can shake, others that show weaknesses here and there.

But rise with the same speed that perhaps comes to fall and those that live stretched out in the gutter of sadness and unhappiness. The modern world brings in the package several psychosomatic evils that evolve and lead the man of that generation to be born, grow and reach old age hunched over with so many emotional woes that, when they don't go crazy, they kill.

There are countless people with psychiatric disorders, mental disorders, suicides, with total or partial loss of reality, all the consequence of the evil of the century that affects large and small, rich and poor, regardless of color, race, religious creed or social position. No one is totally free from the risk of being infected by this evil in their emotions, nor of becoming the next living dead, angry, desperate, lonely, without faith and hope.

Capable of hanging from the neck on a rope. In fact, the more man says to modernize, the more this modernity demands of him and the less capacity he has to comply with so many demands, reaching the height of no longer enduring such pressure, he completely collapses or seeks death as a way out of his terrible emotional suffering. This is the sad end of a society enslaved by skepticism and which insists on living apart from God.

What is Solitude?

This is the most harmful feeling for us who were born with the extreme need to socially relate, directly affecting our emotional, psychological, spiritual and even physical structure, because by its influence we acquire serious symptoms that start to act in all areas of our existence .

Therefore, avoiding this is essential so that we can always be well with life and, thus, face any obstacle during our journey with optimism and the certainty that, in the end, we will overcome difficulties and reach our ideals. Happy people are more resistant to having to go through moments of intense trial. The lonely, depressed, rebellious and bitter with themselves will be easily overcome by the anguish of not being able to reach the top of the mountain. Let's join forces now to completely remove this EVIL OF THE CENTURY.

That has led to increasing numbers of people committing suicide or conditions of extreme isolation and madness

How to Avoid Loneliness?

Living as a family, creating good friendships, visiting public places more often and not discarding a good chat, living a great passion and giving space to a wide smile whenever possible.

Are attitudes that we must all take to escape loneliness. Those who, by choice or need, spend most of their time isolated inside their homes, whether in front of the TV, reading or writing a book, in an online game or browsing social media are likely to fall into the clutches of this number one enemy of human happiness.

Running away from these routine situations at all costs makes it very easy for us to be constantly toasted against this feeling that like cancer corrodes the soul and suffocates our spirits. I recently read an article on the web, where the author stated that science concludes that highly intelligent people are the most lonely and I fully agreed with this recent scientific conclusion.

As a writer I spend a large part of my time in front of a computer creating new works and then publishing them to my thousands of readers, whether on social networks, blogs or through books. That way I ended up joining a monotonous existence and without space for new friendships. There was a period when I was overwhelmed by depression and the best way I found at that moment to get around my sad reality was to seek the company of two old enemies of physical and mental health, alcohol and tobacco. For months I shared my work with an increasing number of beers and cigarettes that consumed me more than helped to change that depressive state.

Finally, I realized that I had gone the wrong way and made bad choices, I gathered strength and gave a "fasta over there" to those with whom I shared my need for social life for a while, quitting addictions, turning off the computer and choosing leave the house more often to breathe fresh air, meet people, go to the mall to shop, go to the cinema or just walk the trails among the dozens of trees in the woods of my city.

Today I feel totally recovered, cured of the evil that I myself created by isolating myself from the outside world, from people, confining myself to a life of work without any leisure or fun. We must consider the following truth: Loneliness is a destructive feeling, but it will only reach us if we open the door for it to enter.

How does depression develop?

A depressive state comes to exist in the human being from the following existential conditions:

— Extreme loneliness

— Deep disappointment

— Total rejection (loving, social or family)

— Huge poverty

— Living on the margins of society

Individuals in these conditions end up contracting a feeling of inferiority that after growing immensely inside their hearts affects the mind to the point of making them believe they are disposable, worthless in the eyes of other people and this leads to despair, isolation and ultimately make extreme decisions like seeking death in order to free yourself from such suffering.

I know a man who fought bravely to fulfill his dream of becoming a great businessman and finally managed to associate with a person with whom he founded a great company. However, after a few years, he discovered that he was being victimized by betrayal by the partner who diverted millions.

To a personal account without this being noticed in time to prevent the company from getting into debt and going into the red. Unable to pay his creditors, that poor man had to sell his share to the unfaithful partner, since he was no longer in any condition to maintain the company on his own.

Today, he lives in an irreversible depressive state, he suffered two heart attacks accompanied by strokes that paralyzed part of his body, all because of the revolt of seeing everything he achieved being taken from his hands.

Without doing anything. That unhappy dream ran down the drain because he trusted the wrong person. I witnessed such a fact in the life of an evangelical pastor, my friend and brother in the faith, after after decades of prosperous pastoral ministry in which he gained high status, becoming an important preacher, administrator and spiritual leader.

He was terribly betrayed by his colleagues and ended up being expelled from his duties accused of illicit acts, but even today without any evidence that would give truth to the accusations, and his end was to live thrown in the gutter — literally speaking.— After being absurdly betrayed by those who said they were brothers in the faith, he was still abandoned by his wife and it ended up being too much for his heart, falling to the bottom of a well from which he has never been able to leave.

Three years ago, the wife of a friend I worked with for several years committed suicide after he announced his desire to part with her. The marriage was not going well and he chose to join another woman and the shock was not borne by that woman who never loved another man in his entire life, he was his first and only great love. So, one day he was at work and received a call from his eldest son, then eighteen years old, reporting that when he got home he found his mother hanging from his neck by a rope.

The terrible death left my friend in shock and this brought him devastating consequences, because, knowing that his mother committed suicide because he threatened to abandon her, his children hated him, both families despised him and today he divides his time between a sip and another of cachaça in the middle of a group of drunks at the tavern on the corner. We must understand that most of the tragedies that have occurred in our lives come from our own attitudes and can be avoided.

A Brief Concept of Happiness

It is very difficult for anyone to draw a complete concept about happiness, since we all little understand what it is to be happy, however, it becomes quite easy to describe unhappiness because we know that it is related to the feeling.

Of pain, sadness, defeat, incapacity, hopelessness, lack of love and everything else that leads to emotional despair. There are many who pretend to be happy by expressing a forced, yellow and false smile in front of those who watch them, but it is enough to see them isolated for a minute, far from the others who perceive the bitterness of sadness in their faces.

A wide smile does not always indicate traces of happiness, sometimes it only serves as a mask to hide deep wounds that exist in someone's soul or heart.

The human being has learned to mask what they really feel or are in front of the world around them because modern society insists on saying that successful and fully realized individuals in financial, social and family life must be completely happy. There are still those who, being extremely religious, claim to have constant happiness because God allows them to do so.

These, as irrational, forget that even Jesus Christ was saddened and wept, lived in despair during the yearning for death and for the pain of the nails that held his body in that rough cross. No one will go through this life without experiencing unhappiness and all its manifestations.

Being happy does not mean never stop smiling, never cry, never feel a deep pain in the chest, not be disappointed or fail, but knowing how to go through all this and more with optimism.

Believing that tomorrow will be better than today and that it will be possible to overcome all the difficulties encountered along the way. Optimistic people tend to achieve greater peace of mind because they trust a better future, but pessimists suffer in advance when visualizing in their minds, seared by the fear of failure, their own defeats. Happiness is a feeling that spreads throughout the body of the person who owns it, in the likeness of a tree whose roots spread beneath the earth without anyone being able to see them.

Reaching the heart and transmitting peace to the previously tired and distressed soul. We can, yes, be happy without a wide laugh on the lips, without material wealth, a lot of money in the bank account or fame and successes. The greatest example of this are dozens of famous people who have committed suicide, claiming depression.

Really happy people do not get depressed or look for a way out of their problems in death, but they are dynamic to the point of facing the adversities of life with courage and determination always get where they want to go without waning. There is a huge contrast in these expressions of human emotion, because while the one who opens a wide smile can bring deep sadness within himself, those who show a fallen face may be feeling fulfilled.

And immensely satisfied with themselves. I remember still in my youth meeting a girl who lived singing in the halls of the school where we studied and for everyone she was the happiest person in the world and in fact it was because she had an unshakable faith.

It was after we started dating and visited her home that I realized that it was possible to hide the shame of poverty and hunger behind a mask of laughter and false joys. That teenager belonged to a very poor family, they lived in a shack with walls made of raw clay.

And covered with straw taken from babassu palms. There was very little furniture inside: a pot instead of the fridge, a homemade stove made of clay. A table with chairs made of coarse wood and a bunch of shame-worthy lumps.

However, without any ceremony she invited me to come in, sit down and have a delicious coffee. He introduced me to his parents, the six younger siblings and in no time stopped singing and smiling, reminding me of the dream of one day becoming a great singer.

Incredible as it may seem recently, we found ourselves on social media after thirty-four years without the slightest contact and to my surprise she now resides in São Paulo. She did not become a professional singer, but a successful businesswoman.

Recalling her miserable past, she said that despite her difficult life, she never lost her faith that she was born in this world to win and conquer the impossible, for this reason she had enough strength to never give up fighting. As I said earlier, truly happy people are optimistic, dynamic, believers and full of security even in the face of the greatest challenges. Only the unfortunate are weak, pessimistic, negative and cowardly when they face the difficulties they encounter along the way. I'm not sure what your situation is right now, we don't even know each other.

But if you are reading this book it is because you need help to understand yourself, life, the world, the other people with whom you relate ... It needs the strength to get up off the ground and continue on an apparently difficult walk or perhaps just to better situate itself in this universe of doubts and interpersonal conflicts.

So follow this example, understand that being happy does not mean living free of problems or totally shielded from the adversities of life, but knowing how to pass through the road of stones and thorns without murmuring, without fear, without fear, fully confident that you were born to win , because only those who do not fight, those who do not face the obstacle with faith and determination and are looking behind or on the ground.

Forgetting that their dream can be right after the first corner, are losers. Let us lift our heads, for our victory will come from above. The same God who gave the life of his only Son on the Cross of Calvary to save us from our crimes and sins will see to it that we arrive at the end of our journey with the guarantee that we will come out unscathed in the most troubled moments of our existence, just for that. trust him and rest in his arms.

The exhausting routine that forces us to run tirelessly from side to side every day, whether because of work.

Studies, different commitments often prevents us from taking a moment to reflect more calmly on what we can do to achieve greater pleasure in life, taking away our inner peace. It is necessary to put an end to this way of being suffocating, extremely exhausting and meaningless, because there is no point in so much struggle.

So much wear and tear, when in the end what will remain will be just the fatigue of another week without good results and little growth in all areas in which we operate, since it is destiny itself that will determine our evolution, be it in the social, emotional and even spiritual realms. If we want to be happy, we must first of all understand that it does not manifest itself to those who live knocking on your door, but to those who know how to wait patiently for their arrival in their lives, even in a dense battle.

Concepts About Love

It is the most pure, clean, true and worthy feeling that a human being can bring within him. Jesus once told his listeners that we should give others what we would like to receive (Matthew 7:12) which indicates that love is free from any selfishness. Those who are selfish will never be able to truly love, because they will only think about achieving their own happiness.

And will not consider the needs of others, whether material, spiritual or affective. To love is to give oneself to someone or to some cause in favor of many, with sincerity and without reservations.

So with the Eternal Father he gave his only Son as a ransom for our souls, we, too, must follow his example and sacrifice ourselves for our fellow men, giving them part of our time to help them with what we have so that we can see them happy.

Jesus Christ is the Son God, he left his kingdom of glory and came down to this world, incarnated in the form of man and suffered everything just so that today we could all be freed from our crimes and sins, receiving once again the right to be reconciled with our Creator.

His death on the Calvary Cross may have been in vain for the most skeptical, unbelievers see him only as a prophet who wanted to show his heroic act before a bewildered crowd, but we who believe what the Holy Scriptures teach us about his divinity we know that he is God, he died and rose on the third day and gave us the greatest proof of love that a human being could have left us. When we live love fully, it transforms us, makes us more dignified, more just, more enlightened people. No one will be able to be fully realized in all areas of their life if they do not allow this feeling to come to their hearts.

Nothing can be more real and true.

Love is an Antidote Against Loneliness

In most visits made to the psychologist during the psychoanalysis sessions, you always hear the same tips on how to avoid lonely life, such as: "Make new friends, frequent more public spaces where there is a greater presence of people, interact, access social networks and share experiences, avoid isolation, get out from behind the four walls.

"But at the end of this list of tips that really contribute a little to the escape from loneliness we need to understand that it is not something material, physical. Not palpable, but a feeling that arises inside the human heart and suffocates the soul like a black cloud, darkening everything around, it comes from the inside and it is not possible to contain it only with certain healthy habits of living together.

An individual's emotional can only be corrected with a more intense feeling, stronger than what he is feeling at the time of his existence. The greatest proof of this is that we can be surrounded by friends, family, in the hottest places and still feel completely alone.This is only due to the fact that sadness is moving within us and not through the streets.

 Squares, museums, cinemas or public places other than our cities. So little in the other people we deal with. Love is undoubtedly the most powerful antidote for curing unhappiness and its symptoms, such as sadness and unwillingness to live. When we love even nature seems to be greener, more colorful and life becomes more interesting.

But let us pay attention to a primary factor in this particular topic: The feeling that heals loneliness, destroys sadness and gives us new perspectives on living is not that disguised passion that many confuse with true love and generally found among couples in love .I speak here of true love, that which comes from above, the same meaning and practiced by Jesus during his earthly ministry for the benefit of all humanity.

Who was able to lead him to endure a terrible death on the Cross and suffer so that today we can join him in one faith and in the future be with him for eternity (Daniel 7:18) We are talking about the sacrificial and divine love that we all carry registered inside our chest as soon as we are born, written down by the fist of God Himself who brought us to life (Romans 2:15)

And that we only need to wake him up and then release him in our actions of charity and mercy towards our neighbor who cries out for help. This love will have a transforming effect on us.

which will root loneliness and its harmful effects on our hearts.

How to Practice Love?

1. Generosity — One of the most common faces of loving our fellow men is the practice of generosity, because through it we can express how much we love people and are happy to help them.

God, our Father and the greatest example of goodness, makes use of this factor every day in allowing us to live, to be healthy to earn our livelihood, for the booklets that allow us to return safely home after a long and tiring period of work and the forgiveness that grants us whenever we repent and to him we confess our faults in a sincere way and without masks.

2. Mercy — Despite the similarity these two faces of love are different from each other, for while one grants sacrificial help to our neighbor, the other has the main characteristic of forgiveness at any cost, without demands or demands. It is easy to open your lips and tell someone that she is forgiven, but to keep in deep anger at the injustice or evil suffered by that person who now repents and comes to apologize. However, in the likeness of our Heavenly Father, we must practice mercy and be able to forgive without leaving roots of bitterness in our hearts.

3. Kindness — To be good is to be charitable, pious, to have compassion for the pain of others. When the Lord looked from the high heavens and saw the degrading way in which man was on earth, due to his bondage to sin, he felt compassion and sent his Son to give him a perfect, holy, spotless sacrifice, so that be accepted and pay the ransom for the soul of the man who was spiritually dead. Kindness leads us to sympathize with the suffering of others.

4. Donation — Knowing whether to donate to our fellow human beings without reservation or any other source of interest other than their complete happiness is also one of the faces of true and divine love.

Personal giving consists in the individual always showing himself ready to help other people, whether financially or in a social work, either within his church or in the community in general.

The most popular cases where we can witness spontaneous donation occur when the population mobilizes and provides voluntary assistance to those who become victims of natural disasters, wars, epidemics and in several other chaotic situations. The act of allowing yourself to serve free of charge to those in need of help is one of several ways of expressing true and pure love in a world full of hatred and prejudice.

5. Breaking Bread — It might not be necessary to mention this particular point, since mercy has already been talked about, however, there is something different between sympathizing and being able to share what we have with our most needy peers.

We are all capable of feeling sorry for those who are being wronged, in financial misery, under pain and suffering, but few have the gift of knowing how to share bread with those in need.

Perhaps you yourself, who read this text about sincere love, I have already visualized the suffering of someone and even felt moved by their anguish, however, you did nothing to change that situation, as I said earlier, it is easy to sympathize.

But it is not always so simple to give part of what we have to others, especially those we don't even know. During one of his many sermons, Jesus was asked by a rich young man what he should do so that after death his soul could have guarantees of salvation and go to paradise.The Master's answer made him very sad.

As he told him to sell all his goods and divide among the poor (Mark 10: 17-25). Then the Lord said that hardly anyone who has material wealth will reach the Kingdom of Heaven.

More About God's Pure Love

1 John 4: 7 [7] *Beloved, let us love one another; because love is from God; and anyone who loves is born of God and knows God*.

Faith is expressed by love. Love for the Lord, love for His Word, love for our brothers ... We become like Jesus when we put love first and that is fantastic. The closer we get to Jesus, the more we become like Him, we start to see the world from another perspective.

We love people for no reason, we have a compassion that we can't even explain where it came from. The closer we are to Jesus, the more of him we have in us, it is a fact. Love is a fruit of the Spirit and did you know that the greatest aspect of the fruits is love of neighbor?

Sometimes it can be difficult to love the other, to set aside differences, but the Holy Spirit puts it inside us and it is inevitable. There is no way to resist and to love is also to serve. We are living in difficult times and we need to take good care of those we love.

Taking care of yourself at that moment is also a way of loving. It is necessary to have a lot of responsibility to deal with everything that is happening in the World.

Faith Awakens God's Love for His Children

Mark 5: 27-28 [27] *Hearing about Jesus, he came from behind the crowd and touched his dress. [28] Because he said: If I just touch your dresses, I will heal.*

I believe that you must have heard of the story of the Woman of the Blood Flow during the preaching at the church where she attends. In my years of walking, I saw countless ministries about this story and I can say with conviction that even though the same text the Lord spoke to my heart in different ways every time I heard it. Funny how the Bible is.

This happens frequently to me. I read the same text and every time I reread it, I notice points that I hadn't seen before. The Faith of the woman of the blood flow is very inspiring. She was already desperate because of her condition ...He spent everything he had, used every means, and when he finally heard of Jesus, he still found the strength to trust. She planned her action, exercised her Faith, touched Jesus' garments and was HEALED.

That woman had been bleeding for twelve years. Imagine what she had to go through, the shame, the countless unsuccessful attempts at healing ... Maybe she had no more hope.

But when she heard about Jesus she had an attitude of Faith and went in search of his miracle. Our personal Faith is very important to God and has the power to move his hands in our favor, to awaken his immense love for us.

I don't know what your struggles are, I don't know what your "blood flow" is, but I know that believing is the certainty of what we can still see and even if you still can't see your miracle happen., Trust him! Put your problems in Jesus' hands.

I Thessalonians 1: 6 [6] **And you were made our imitators, and of the Lord, receiving the word in much tribulation, with the joy of the Holy Spirit.**

All of us must be imitators of Christ and for that we must delve into the Word to know him. There are three attributes of Jesus to get to know this loving God better, because our goal must be like Him.

1. Love — Love is an evidence of Faith in Jesus, it is only through love that we can see it visibly in this world. Jesus loved without looking at whom he loved, instructed, rebuked and cared for. When we can love as Jesus loves, then we know him better.

2. Meekness — Meekness is very similar to patience.

And what is different about them? Meekness is the state of mind of someone who has control and control over their temperament and attitudes, a calm person who can handle things without aggression of any kind. Patience, on the other hand, is the virtue of those who endure evils and annoyances without complaints or revolt. It is to endure hostility without anger.

In addition to being patient, Jesus resolved his conflicts with meekness. He always resolved his conflicts smoothly and remained calm. He was fully aware that his Words and Attitudes had a weight and that people have feelings and that is why he always acted in the best possible way. When we can be meek as Jesus was, to learn to deal with people and situations just as He did.

3. Self-control — We need to have self-control so that we do not let our human and carnal nature get out of control. It is to have dominion over yourself so as not to fall into temptations. Jesus was tempted countless times in the desert and not once did He fall. He had dominion and won over the proposals that the enemy put in front of him. These are not just characteristics of Jesus, but fruits of the Spirit that we must seek. Jesus is our mirror.

How to Be Happy Despite Afflictions?

Think of how many people are currently in hospital beds immensely ill or even condemned to death; others behind bars in a chain and those who looked at their pantries without finding even one type of food to eat. Think of the slandered, unjustly condemned people and those who are now thinking of committing suicide ...

Now analyze your current situation and ask yourself if despite the regrets it is not much better than the examples given above. Sometimes we wake up in the morning angry because we have not yet achieved the fulfillment of our most desired dreams, such as buying a car of the year, making that long-planned trip, renovating our homes or becoming a father and mother, receiving a promotion at work. , a pay raise...If we stop to think we will see that all this is nothing compared to the situation in which many other people are at that.

Moment and that if we think more clearly we will see that we have plenty of reasons to wake up every day after a wonderful night of sleep and glorify ourselves to God for his care for us. We are alive, healthy, our family is well and we have food in the pot. Is this so little for us that it does not deserve a glory to God and a wide smile on our lips?

What happens is that we are few thanked for what we are and have, we murmur instead of knowing that we value what we have.

We are what we think

Parapsychology is the area of science that studies the human mind and it says that we have power in our thoughts capable of changing the world around us. In fact, this mental force that science calls "Positive Thinking" is nothing more than the "Power of Faith" that Christ revealed to us in the Gospels (Mark 9:23).

According to his teachings "everything is possible for those who believe". That is, if we firmly believe that something will happen in our lives it will eventually materialize and will actually happen as we think. I remember that, when I was still young, I kept telling my colleagues that I would be a diabetic in maturity because that was how it was with my father.

The grandfather, the great-grandfather. As soon as I reached the age of fifty, the disease manifested itself as I had predicted. However, I came to believe that I would find a way to be cured, even though medicine says there is no cure for this disease. Recently a doctor and scientist developed a formula that guarantees the immediate cure of this type of deficiency in the body.

And when starting the treatment my blood glucose rate dropped instantly from two hundred and fifty to ninety as a miracle. What we can see is that my health is being controlled by my thoughts, when I imagined myself a victim of this serious illness it simply appeared in my life and when I believed in my recovery I immediately found the cure that everyone said did not exist.

If, according to Christ, everything is possible to believe, then we must seek to believe in the best for our lives and that of our families. I don't know what the reader is facing at the moment, but I recommend that you always seek to attract the best in life with thoughts that make you happy.

Be Someone Enlightened

There are two types of people in this world we inhabit: the enlightened and the children of darkness.

1. Illuminated — All those individuals who transmit positive, constructive energy to others are able to help them move forward with faith and optimism. Light-filled people never express demotivating words.

Or attitudes that take their listeners or observers down, because they reflect a force that pushes everyone and everything upwards. It is essential that we seek the company of these individuals in our social life as a whole.

Their friendship will do us good and will help us to find ways to continue taking long strides towards the future driven by their incentives. Such friends will always give us full support when talking to them about our most daring projects and in no way will they discourage us or see any difficulties that may hinder our journey. Enlightened people are positive, optimistic, believers, full of confidence and at no time will they tell us to step back in the face of a challenge.

2. The Children of Darkness — Unlike the enlightened, this class of people lives dominated by pessimism and lives looking backwards or downwards. They are unbelievers, negative, blasphemous and never believe in their own potentials. In this way, they doubt the ability that someone may have to fight and conquer their highest ideals, always trying to put them down, taking their strength.

It is extremely necessary to avoid an intimate or extreme relationship with this type of person, as we can be influenced by their negativity and gradually lose our inner light, failing to believe in ourselves. Let us approach God through the faith he has given us and stay as far away as possible from the "Children of Darkness"

Personality Flaws

Each person has their own flaws or personality qualities in particular, below we will see the most important ones for this study:

1. Pride — Proud people can hardly perceive or accept the good qualities that exist in other people, in their conception only they shine in their attitudes, that is, only their actions are worthy of praise and deserve exaltation.

Such individuals tend to isolate themselves, their lives become empty and lonely due to the fact that their eyes belittle most of the friendships they could win because they feel superior to the others around them.

2. Malice — Malicious people are people with a tendency to destructive criticism, the kind who stay at a distance just making fun of the actions taken by others, pointing out their possible failures or failures.

For these, no one will ever do anything worthy of praise or applause, for them all are incapable, weak, unworthy of respect. They do not support their peers, are suspicious by nature and do not miss a chance to criticize, speak ill, condemn and disparage anyone.

3. Envy — Envious people feel unable to achieve their dreams or carry out their life projects.

And in this way feel revolted when they see that others have arrived there, where they think they will never succeed. Such people are moved by the same sentiment as the Devil, when he looked up and wished to sit on the throne of the Most High because he thinks he is more important than the Creator Himself (Ezekiel 28: 13-19).

And will do everything to prevent his reach the top of their achievements. They live surrounded by darkness, are revolted, bitter, critical, pessimistic, their tongue continually harsh condemns the attitudes of others, when they themselves do not behave decently. However, they will be destroyed, overcome by the very envy that will consume them. Because just like Lucifer they will dig their own tomb and fall into the very hole they prepared for those who bitterly desired to destroy.

4. The Lie — Liars delight in making up false stories for their listeners in order to draw their attention to themselves or to promote themselves. It is common to hear people who report having accomplished great things in life, when in reality they never even came close to practicing such things. The liar is someone who inwardly feels weak, small in front of the world and other people and tries to be important.

5. Slander — Slanderers resemble liars.

But there is a huge difference in their attitudes. While the former is only intended to be perceived and accepted by those who listen to it, the latter aims to defame someone innocent and destroy his reputation, however, slanderers have in common with liars the weakness found in the Devil.

The word "Satan" means "Accuser". Therefore, every slanderer is a Satan before the eyes of God. According to the Scriptures, the Devil lives day and night before the Most High, accusing the human being and desiring his destruction, because he hates man for being the most important Creation of the Almighty. He lived in Eden full of glory and light, he wanted to ascend to the heavens and become the dominator of the entire universe.

But he was thrown down with the angels who followed him in that rebellion (Revelation 12: 7-9). For having been humiliated, expelled from paradise and living in complete darkness, today he tries to annihilate the children of God because his feeling of envy against the chosen ones is so great. In the same way it happens with the envious, they are dominated by the influence of the enemy of God and they start to persecute those who manage to triumph, to win, to shine before their eyes. They are failed, losers and frustrated people.

6. Hate — Hateful people do not find peace or contribute to others finding it, nothing is worse than living with these types of people.

55

Solomon in the splendor of his wisdom made an analogy between the contentious woman and the trickle of raindrops. He said:

"The continuous dripping in a day of great rain, and the contentious woman, both are similar" Proverbs 27:15 . It is prudent on our part to avoid joining with these people because they will never allow us a single day of happiness, as they are dissatisfied, quarrelsome, bitter, pessimistic, negative and rejoice in evil.

7. The Grudge — The grudges are never at ease with life or with their fellow men, they keep guarding the hurts of those who may hurt their heels. They do not know how to forgive or are interested in appeasing broken relationships.

They view friendship with disdain and consider all those who speak the truth to them or show their mistakes as mortal enemies. Staying away from the spiteful ones is a wise choice of existence for those who aspire to be happy in this world, as this is the best way to avoid coming into strife with such individuals and to buy a fight that will last forever, since they never forget one. affront.

8. Pornography — Sexual immorality is something extremely harmful to our lives.

But unfortunately in the modern world we live in, with full access to technology, with the virtual world in the palm of our hands, we are hardly tempted to take a look behind the curtain and follow our more audacious carnal instincts.

Young people, teenagers, men and women of all ages have at some point stopped to take a look at porn videos available on the internet and contaminated their eyes, stained their hearts with sin and sexual immorality. Nowadays doing these things is considered normal, since these media are freely available to anyone who wants to have access.

However, in the Scriptures Paul asks those who already know Christ to avoid contaminating themselves with any form of sin, purifying their mind, body and spirit while they await his coming.

"But you did not learn Christ in this way, if you have heard him, and have been taught in him, as is the truth in Jesus. That, as for the past treatment, you dispose of the old man, who is corrupted by the lusts of deception and is renewed in the spirit of your mind.

And put on the new man, who according to God is created in true justice and holiness. Therefore, leave the lie, and speak the truth each with your neighbor.

Because we are members of each other. Be angry, and do not sin; do not let the sun go down on your anger. Give no place to the devil.

He who stole, don't steal anymore; rather work, doing with your hands what is good, so that you have something to share with what you need.

No nasty words will come out of your mouth, but only the one that is good for promoting the building, so that it will give grace to those who hear it.

And do not grieve the Holy Spirit of God, in whom you are sealed for the day of redemption. All bitterness, and anger, and anger, and shouting, and blasphemy, and all malice, be taken away from you,

Rather be kind and merciful to one another, forgiving one another, just as God forgave you in Christ". Ephesians 4: 20-32

The Fruits of Human Meat

Skeptics claim that we are formed only of matter, but the Word of God says that we are body, soul and spirit. Human flesh came from the dust of the earth as we read in Genesis 2: 7 and therefore has nowhere to do with the spiritual, that is, when it dies it will return to dust and for this reason it is not concerned with salvation or eternal condemnation. In other words: To understand clearly how this occurs.

Let us think of an extremely selfish person who only cared about his own interests. Therefore, it would not matter to her whether A or B goes bad in life as long as she is in good shape herself. Well, this is how things work between our physical body and the soul, he has his own desires and wants to satisfy them at any cost with little regard for the harmful results that this will have on him.

It turns out that this very soul that we are talking about here is us, spiritual beings that inhabit within physical bodies. Imagine your naked body that needs clothes to be able to leave the house and become presentable to other people, well, so it is in relation to our spiritual being.

The soul (us) is invisible and can only relate visibly in this world if it has a physical body. It happens that, if we don't watch over the clothes we wear, it gets dirty, rots, tears and ends. So it is with the body, we need to take care of it so that nothing bad happens to it.

Feed it, maintain hygiene, keep it away from drugs, addictions and not allow it to dominate us (the soul), causing us to commit excess of sins that when we leave it and return to the world of spirits we have a high price to pay in front of the one who allowed us to live in this world. Paul, the apostle, in his letter written to the brothers in the Galatians church, warned:

"Because you, brothers, have been called to freedom. Do not then use your freedom to give occasion to the flesh, but serve one another out of love. For the whole law is fulfilled in one word, in this: You will love your neighbor as yourself.

But if you bite and devour one another, see that you do not consume one another as well. I say, however: Walk in the Spirit, and you will not fulfill the lust of the flesh.

Because the flesh lusts against the Spirit, and the Spirit against the flesh; and they are opposed to each other, lest you do what you want. But if you are guided by the Spirit, you are not under the law. Because the works of the flesh are manifest, which are: adultery.

Fornication, impurity, lust, Idolatry, witchcraft, enmities, strife, emulations ... Wraths, fights, dissensions, heresies, envies, homicides, drunkenness, gluttonies, and the like, about which I declare to you, as I said before, that those who commit such things will not inherit the kingdom of God.

But the fruit of the Spirit is: love, joy, peace, longsuffering, kindness, goodness, faith, meekness, temperance. Against such there is no law. And those who are Christ's have crucified the flesh with its passions and lusts.

If we live in Spirit, let us also walk in Spirit. Let us not be greedy."
Galatians 5: 13-26

Those who are usually dominated by carnal desires will have to give an account of this to God after physical death, that is, after they leave the body and this will bring eternal condemnation. Anyone who says "the body is mine, I make it what I think is best!"

No, my friends, the body belongs to the God who created it, we are just stewards chosen to live and care for it, but then we will be accountable for what we let it do in this life.

Let us remember this to properly look after the property of others. Regarding the fruits of the Spirit, beneficial to the human body for the well-being of the soul.

Paulo mentions the most important and encourages us to seek them:

"But the fruit of the Spirit is: love, joy, peace, patience, kindness, goodness, faith, meekness, temperance.

Against such there is no law. And those who are Christ's have crucified the flesh with its passions and lusts. If we live in Spirit, let us also walk in Spirit." **Galatians 5: 22-25**

How to Be Socially Accepted

In this world considered modern, although this modernity has not contributed to a significant evolution in the human character, we need to have a game to find space between the different social classes. A person with an orthodox personality is unlikely to find social acceptance with great ease, as he will not be able to please the demands of those who consider debauchery a laudable characteristic.

The human being, in our day, has completely inclined to life without shame and for good people to be accepted in their midst must agree with their cheap ideologies, whoever does not do so will be despised.

An example of this is the current valorization of homosexuality, which has already reached thousands of people regardless of their class or social status. Those who, out of fidelity to their religious faith — or because they have a more dignified character —

Refuse to accept the intimate relationship between people of the same sex because they understand it to be unnatural will be banned from interaction with those who find this type of human condition acceptable. This leads to the creation of new social groups.

On the one hand the most liberal and on the other those who remain in extreme aversion to such practices considered by them as shameful. Even within religions there are divisions among its members, some believe that such people should be accepted in their midst because they believe that God will free them from their moral weaknesses and those who are deeply opposed to such thinking. In addition to homosexuality — considered the worst of human moral conditions — There are several other factors that can influence the decision of a social group to refuse to receive an individual as a new member.

Young people are required to use alcoholic beverages, to consume drugs, to live in a rebellious way, to follow worldly customs ... Otherwise, they may end up isolated in any corner of life because they do not adapt to such demands. But in these cases, we need to remember what the psalmist said: "Because when my father and mother forsake me, the Lord will take me in." *Psalm 27:10*

Segunda Parte

Reflections: Psalm 119: 100

[100] I am more prudent than the old, because I keep your precepts.

The Bible is our instruction manual for having a good life and a life that is ever closer to our Creator. We can find countless principles to follow and adopt as a lifestyle, and today I want to talk about five Fundamental Principles that you need to start practicing immediately:

1. Handle all matters prudently — And what is it? He is a prudent person who is cautious, sensible and does not seek danger or even strife.

We must treat everything prudently, try to be fair and patient. Listen to both sides, try to keep the peace and resolve situations in the best possible way.

2. Be open to instruction — Many people are closed in on their own beliefs and do not accept new opinions or teachings.

This reminds the Pharisees and Sadducees who were not open to the new and therefore did not believe that Jesus was the Messiah. Therefore, we must seek our certainties, but always be open to learn even more.

3. Be an understanding person — All of us we are susceptible to error and should learn from them daily. We cannot judge our brother, after all, we must not judge anyone until the Lord comes. So we must be understanding and try to deal with people and situations prudently.

4. Always speak wisely — There are things that need not be said and a wise person knows what to say - and the best way to speak - at the right time. Try to be a wise person instead of throwing silly words in the wind.

5. Increase your Knowledge — The more we know about God, the more we need to know. We need to yearn for the Word and for knowledge, because that is something that no one can take away from us. Therefore, dedicate yourself to becoming an increasingly wise person, always be grounded in the Word of God, which is the place where the most God speaks to man, and instructs him.

Reflections: Isaiah 53: 4

[4] Truly he took our infirmities upon himself, and took our pains upon himself; and we regarded him as afflicted, wounded by God, and oppressed.

Are your Faith and your love growing?

I will improve my question: Are your Faith in God and your love for your brothers growing?

Yeah, the situation is kind of complicated with this virus, isn't it? What have you been thinking about it?

Isaiah 53 says that Jesus took our pains and OUR ENDINGS!

Psalm 91 assures us that if kept by the Lord, we would not be affected!

Jesus called Peter to walk on water and while he was focused on Christ he walked on water and lived the supernatural, but when he focused on the storm he started to sink.

Our focus defines what we are experiencing. In times of crisis we need to remember what brings us hope.

We need to be with a biblical mentality and keep the Word in our hearts, memorizing passages from Scripture is a bit complicated at times, isn't it?

Do not allow experiences to limit what the Word says.

It says that the Lord not only heals, but that HE IS THE HEALING.

Lift your experiences to biblical truths, like the truth that Jesus says we would do even greater works than He did,

If He healed, you can also bring healing, in His name.

We already have the solution the world needs in the Word and the more biblical texts you have on the tip of your tongue, the more you will be grounded in memorizing the Gospel.

The Word is the way to face all situations and if we are grounded in it, we need not fear any harm. And don't forget:

The Bible foresaw all of these events, and ñ it is because we are children that we must be inconsequential, but we need to trust that the Lord is our strength and very present help in anguish. We need to trust him.

Reflections: II Corinthians 12: 9

[9] And he said to me, My grace is sufficient for you, because my power is perfected in weakness. I willingly boast in my weaknesses, so that the power of Christ may dwell in me.

We see many people living blessed and victorious lives, God did not create us to live in the desert.

He created us to live the best of this land, and that does not mean that we will stop going through struggles, but it does mean that God reserved the best for his children. Today I separated some "secrets" for you and your home to walk in Vitória

1 Stand firm — Stand firm in the Gospel and be free, it was for freedom that Jesus set you free from the bonds of sin. So leave behind your concepts and everything that separates you from the truth of the Gospel. Go on trusting and remember: Faith is the certainty of the things we can see.

2 Be guided by the Holy Spirit — "I no longer live, Christ lives in me".

We are temples of the Holy Spirit and in no way can we live according to the desires of our flesh, we are a new creature and we must be guided by the Spirit.

3 Obey the Word — It's that old phrase "Obeying is better than sacrificing". For the will of God is good, perfect and pleasant. We will not always understand, but He knows what is best for us, trust the God you serve and will walk in victory when he learns to hear His voice and obey His Word.

Reflections: Romans 9: 28

[28] For the Lord will execute his word on the earth, completing and shortening it.

I don't know if you know, but the Bible reports 3 different types of death.

1 Physical Death — The one we know, the separation of the inner man from his body. The body without the Spirit is dead and you can find that in James 2: 26

2 Spiritual Death — This one you probably should also know. This type of death is when man separates himself from God because of sin. In order for this not to happen our Spirit needs to be fed, we need to water our relationship with God every day. Even when we make mistakes we need to have a heart like David's, that when he made mistakes he would tear himself in the presence of God with all sincerity. When you sin, run even closer to the Lord.

3 Eternal Death — This is the Eternal separation between man and God, it is when man chooses to live in sin forever.

It is called the second death. Throughout the Bible death means separation. It is the separation of the purpose for which someone was created.

We need to study more about these subjects in the Bible, because the more we study the more we have to learn. I know we are living in difficult times, make the most of it as much as possible to put things in their right place, seek quality time with your family and take care of each other. Let us feed more on the Bible, dedicate ourselves to delving deeper into the Word of God, in it we seek to have eternal life.

Reflections: Matthew 16: 13-15

[13] And when Jesus came to the parts of Caesarea Philippi, he asked his disciples, saying, Who do men say that I am the Son of man? [14] And they said, Some John the Baptist, some Elijah, and some Jeremiah or one of the prophets. [15] He said to them, "Who do you say I am?"

I've been thinking about how people see Jesus and what He means to them. So I ask you: What is Jesus for you?

For many in the Bible, He was considered the Master, the Lord, the Son of David or just a simple carpenter.

Jesus cannot be just a Teacher For you as Buddha, Gandhi or Dalai Lama, because He never claimed to be a guru. Jesus cannot be just a man who did good or miracles like others. And do you know why?

Because Jesus claimed that he WAS THE SON OF GOD, the way, the truth and the Life. The truth is that at some point you need to make a choice about Jesus. Believing that He is the son of God and is said to believe that He is the incarnate God owes you REVERENCE.

You owe him OBEDIENCE to his precepts or believe that He was a fanatic and risk being the one who rejects God's salvation.

This decision is made every day in our lives and we must not forget to always choose to believe that He is THE SON OF GOD and that His grace is enough for us.

Reflection: Jonah 3: 5

[5] And the men of Nineveh believed in God, and proclaimed a fast, and clothed themselves in sackcloths, from the largest to the smallest.

Today, let's talk a little about fasting. When you hear the word "fast", what comes to your mind? I feel that today the church is divided between two extremes: those who do not value fasting at all and those who exceed expectations about it.

The practice of fasting is not mandatory, but it is a biblical recommendation because it brings with it some principles that must be understood and followed.

Verses like Mt 6: 16-18 talk about how much Jesus expected us to practice fasting. So I want to encourage you to practice fasting for seven reasons:

1- To grow in intimacy with Jesus

2 - To receive wisdom and direction

3 - To receive protection

4 - To experience the power of God

5 - By fulfilling God's promises in our city and nation

6 - To stop a crisis (individual, family or national)

And that is our goal today, a national fast as in Nineveh, at the time of the prophet Jonah, only today we are to cry out to the Lord to free us from this plague that is plaguing the world and giving us prosperity.

7 - For the prophetic revelation of the end times

I like a statement by Kenneth Hagin about fasting:

"Fasting does not change God. He is the same before, during and after his fast. But, fasting will change you. It will help you to remain more susceptible to the Spirit of God ".

I believe that after today there will be a brokenness of the Brazilian people and hearts will be more open to receive Jesus as Savior.

I believe that the primary purpose of fasting is to mortify the flesh, which will make us more susceptible to the Holy Spirit.

Reflections: Genesis 11: 6

[6] And the LORD said, Behold, the people are one, and they all have the same language; and this is what they begin to do; and now there will be no restriction on everything they try to do.

I believe you may have heard of the history of Torre d Babel. But if you haven't heard or remember, I'll refresh your memory a little.

There was a time when all the inhabitants of the Earth spoke the same language and the people decided to come together to build a Tower that would reach Heaven, because they wanted to become famous. Seeing what was happening, God said:

"They all come together and speak the same language. If this is the beginning of what they do, nothing they set out to do from now on will be impossible for them. Come on, let's go down and confuse them with different languages, so that they won't be able to understand each other. ".

And so the Lord scattered them all over the world, and they stopped building the city.

This story became known worldwide and many historians and scientists have already found concrete proof of its veracity. Of course, everything in the Bible is true, but it is great to see science proving the facts. In my opinion this is also a way for skeptics to be reached by the love of God. But I want to talk today about a specific point.

UNITY!

When the people are united, nothing will be impossible before them and that is why Jesus intends to live together. My prayer today is that the Church will have one heart, one purpose and will always walk towards the same goal because in this way we will make a difference in this nation and in the world.

We all have differences, but they can be set aside for a greater purpose. The Tower of Babel existed and leaves us with a great lesson to this day: Let us all be one! And more than ever, this is the time to be ONE! It is time to be united in prayer, time to be firm and confident that the Lord is taking care of everything.

I know that many are afraid, but perfect love casts out all fear and that does not mean that we do not need to take care, but it means that we have someone to trust and we need not fear anything. Take care of yourself and the one you love.

Reflection: Colossians 2: 13-14

[13] And when you were dead in sins, and in the uncircumcision of your flesh, he quickened you together with him, forgiving you of all trespasses, [14] Having crossed out the ballot that was against us in his ordinances, which it was in some way contrary to us, and took it out of us, nailing it to the cross.

There is no greater love than that which Christ feels for us, He paid a price for us that was impossible to pay. When man sinned in the garden, there was a separation between us and God, Jesus came with his infinite love to break paradigms and make us know who God truly is and especially to restore the Covenant that was broken in Eden.

There are a few reasons why Jesus gave himself out of love for you and me, and they are:

1 For our sins — All sin has a consequence and Jesus paid the consequence of all our sins, because the wages of sin is death and Jesus delivered us from the bondage of sin.

It gave us the opportunity to have Eternal Life.

2 For reconciliation — God does not dwell in what is not Holy, with the death of Jesus on the Cross we were redeemed and today we have free access to the Father, we have been reconciled and our covenant with God has been restored. Before Jesus' death, we needed a priest to access God. Today we can be called friends of God and his children.

3 To sanctify the Church by the Word — Jesus was the Word. The Word was with God, the Word was God Himself, the Word became flesh and dwelt among us, and today we have the Word of God, through the Word that is our Manual of Life (alive and effective) Jesus keeps talking and breaking paradigms, through the Bible Jesus continues to transform the Church and prepare it for his return.

Reflection: James 4: 7

[7] Submit yourselves therefore to God, resist the devil, and he will flee from you.

Make Satan know that you are a loser. The more Satan rises, the more precious his victory in Christ will be. The New Testament teaches that when Christ died and rose again, Satan was defeated. His power against God's people has been broken and his destruction is certain.

"For this the Son of God was manifested: to destroy the works of the devil" **(1 John 3: 8).**

Hebrews 2: 14 assures us that: "The death of Christ destroyed the one who has the power of death, namely, the devil". Paul added: "[God,] stripping principalities and powers, publicly exposed them to contempt, triumphing over them on the cross" (Col. 2: 15). In other words, the decisive blow was delivered at Calvary. What does this mean for those who follow Jesus Christ? That "Now, therefore, there is no longer condemnation for those who are in Christ Jesus" (Rom. 8: 1). "Who will bring a charge against the elect of God? It is God who justifies them "(Rom. 8: 33).

"Because I am quite sure that neither death, nor life, nor angels, nor principalities, nor things of the present, nor of the future, nor the powers, nor the height, nor the depth, nor any other creature he will be able to separate us from the love of God, which is in Christ Jesus our Lord "(Rom. 8: 38-39). "Greater is he who is in you than he who is in the world" **(1 John 4: 4).**

"They [the saints] therefore overcame him because of the blood of the Lamb and because of the word of the testimony they gave" (Rev. 12: 11).

Therefore, "resist the devil, and he will flee from you!" He was defeated, and we were given victory. Our task now is to live in that victory and make Satan know his defeat.

Reflexão: Salmos 23: 4

[4] Ainda que eu andasse pelo vale da sombra da morte, não temeria mal algum, porque tu estás comigo; a tbua vara e o teu cajado me consolam.

Falemos com Deus, não apenas sobre ele.

A estrutura do salmo 23 é instrutiva.

Nos três primeiros versículos, Davi se refere a Deus como "Ele":

O SENHOR é o meu pastor…

Ele me faz repousar…

Ele leva-me…

Ele refrigera-me a alma…

Depois, nos versículos 4 e 5, Davi se refere a Deus como "Tu":

Ñ temerei mal nenhum, pq tu estás comigo;

Teu bordão e o teu cajado me consolam.

Tu me preparas uma mesa…

Tu me unges a cabeça com óleo.

Então, no versículo 6 ele volta p/ a terceira pessoa:

Eu habitarei na Casa do SENHOR.

A lição que aprendemos a partir dessa estrutura é que não é bom falar muito tempo sobre Deus sem falar com Deus.

Todo cristão é, no mínimo, um teólogo amador — ou seja, uma pessoa que tenta compreender o caráter e os caminhos de Deus e depois colocar isso em palavras. Se não somos pequenos teólogos, então não diremos nada uns aos outros sobre Deus e seremos de pouquíssima ajuda para a fé de nossos ouvintes.

Porém, o que aprendemos com Davi no Salmo 23 é que nós deveríamos entrelaçar nossa teologia com oração. Deveríamos frequentemente interromper nossa conversa sobre Deus para falarmos sobre ele aos que ouvem. Não muito depois da afirmação teológica "Deus é generoso", deve vir a afirmação como oração: "Graças te dou, Senhor". Junto a "Deus é glorioso", deve vir: "Eu louvo a tua glória". O que podemos perceber é que essa é a maneira que deve ser, se é que estamos sentindo a realidade de Deus em nossos corações, assim como estamos descrevendo-a com nossas cabeças.

Reflection: Psalm 23: 4

[4] Even if I walked through the valley of the shadow of death, I would fear no harm, because you are with me; your stick and your staff comfort me.

Let's talk to God, not just about him.

The structure of Psalm 23 is instructive.

In the first three verses, David refers to God as "He":

The Lord is my shepherd…

He makes me rest ...

He takes me ...

It cools my soul ...

Then, in verses 4 and 5, David refers to God as "You":

I will fear no harm, because you are with me;

Your staff and your staff comfort me.

You prepare a table for me ...

You anoint my head with oil.

Then, in verse 6 he goes back to the third person:

I will dwell in the house of the LORD.

The lesson we learn from this structure is that it is not good to talk about God for a long time without talking to God.

Every Christian is, at the very least, an amateur theologian - that is, a person who tries to understand the character and ways of God and then put it into words. If we are not little theologians, then we will not say anything to each other about God and we will be of little help to the faith of our listeners.

However, what we learned from David in Psalm 23 is that we should intertwine our theology with prayer. We should often interrupt our conversation about God in order to tell those who hear about Him. Not long after the theological statement *"God is generous", the statement must come as a prayer: "Thank you, Lord." Next to "God is glorious", it must come: "I praise your glory".* What we can see is that this is the way it should be, if we are feeling the reality of God in our hearts, just as we are describing it with our heads.

Reflection: Matthew 5: 44

[44] But I say to you, Love your enemies, bless those who curse you, do good to those who hate you, and pray for those who mistreat you and persecute you.

What does it mean to pray for your enemy? Prayer for your enemies is one of the most profound ways of showing love, because it means that we really want something good to happen to them.

You can do pleasant things for your enemies without any genuine desire that things will go well with them. However, prayer for them occurs in the presence of God who knows your heart when you pray and intercede for God on their behalf.

Prayer can be for their conversion, for repentance, so that they are awakened to the evil in their hearts and are set free. It may be that they are interrupted in their downward spiral of sin, even if illness or tragedy does so. But the prayer that Jesus has in mind here is always for their sake.

This is what Jesus did while he was hanging on the cross:

"Father, forgive them, because they do not know what they are doing" **(Luke 23: 34).**

And this is what Stephen did when he was being stoned:

"Then, kneeling down, he cried out with a loud voice: Lord, do not impute this sin to them!" (Acts 7: 60).

Jesus is calling us ñ just to do good things for our enemies, such as greeting them and helping to meet their needs; he is also calling us to wish the best for them and to express those wishes in prayers when the enemy is not present.

Our hearts must desire your salvation, want your presence in heaven and long for your eternal happiness. Thus, we pray like the apostle Paul for the Jewish people, many of whom made life very difficult for Paul: *"My heart's good will and my plea to God are for them to be saved"* (Rom. 10: 1)

Human Egoism

"Our ego is sitting on the throne of our heart and does not want to leave it for anything, not even to give place to God, who is the only one who has the right to occupy it. And this tyrant who is seated on this throne is demanding, vain, proud and sly; and makes us suffer "- By Prof. Felipe Aquino

After Satan convinced Adam and Eve to rebel against divine ordinances and led them to sin, allowing evil to enter this world, the human heart became hardened to the point of causing man to no longer hear the voice of his Creator nor accept to obey his advice. Jeremiah spoke to us wisely about this in his writings centuries ago when he lent his lips to the Spirit of the Lord, and so we read:

"Why, then, do these people of Jerusalem turn away with such a continuous apostasy? Persists in deception, does not want to return.

I heard and heard; they do not speak what is right, there is no one to repent of their wickedness, saying: What have I done? Each one deviates in his career, like a horse that throws with impetus in the battle. Even the stork in the sky knows its set times.

And the dove, and the crane and the swallow watch the time of their coming; but my people do not know the judgment of the Lord. How then do you say, We are wise, and the law of the Lord is with us? Behold, the false pen of the scribes has been working in vain.Wise men are ashamed, astonished and imprisoned; behold, they have rejected the word of the Lord; what wisdom, then, do they have? Jeremiah 8: 5-9

In the words quoted by the prophet we see the sadness of God when he saw that his people had turned their backs on him and were trying to live alienated from his Law, satisfying his own insane desires, denying his existence as Sovereign over their heads.

They grew tired of his advice and began to doubt whether he was in fact real as Moses and the other leaders who preceded him said, after all, they never saw him face to face.

Nowadays things are no different, because God is invisible and presents himself to man only through faith has become for many just a fairy tale, a legend or superstition created by Christians.

However, all those who wish to know him truly through the person of Christ will experience an incomparable joy of peace and spiritual comfort, accompanied by the assurance of eternal life.

This apostasy of the present century had already been announced more than two thousand years ago by Jesus and his apostles. Paul warned his disciple Timothy:

"But the Spirit expressly says that in recent times some of the faith will apostatize, listening to deceiving spirits.

And the doctrines of demons. For the hypocrisy of men who speak lies, having their own conscience seared." **1 Timothy 4: 1,2**

Peter, for his part, warned about this:

"And there were also false prophets among the people, just as there will be false doctors among you, who will covertly introduce heresies of perdition, and will deny the Lord who redeemed them, bringing upon themselves sudden perdition.

And many will follow their dissolutions, by which the way of truth will be blasphemed. And out of greed they will make a deal of you with false words; on which for a long time the sentence will not be late, and their perdition does not sleep. For if God did not forgive the angels who sinned, but, having cast them into hell, he gave them up to the chains of darkness, being reserved for judgment.

And he did not forgive the ancient world, but kept Noah, the eighth person, the preacher of justice, by bringing the flood over the world of the wicked.

And he condemned the cities of Sodom and Gomorrah to destruction, reducing them to ash, and setting an example for those who lived wickedly.

And he freed just Lot, bored with the dissolute life of abominable men

(Because this righteous man, living among them, afflicted his righteous soul every day, so he saw and heard about his unjust works).

Thus does the Lord know how to deliver the pious from temptation, and reserve the unjust for the day of judgment, to be punished. But mainly those who, according to the flesh, walk in filthy lusts, and despise the authorities; bold, obstinate, not afraid to blaspheme dignities.

While the angels, being greater in strength and power, do not pronounce blasphemous judgment against them before the Lord.

But these, like irrational animals, who follow nature, made to be arrested and killed, blaspheming what they do not understand, will perish in their corruption. Receiving the reward of injustice; since such men take pleasure in daily delights, they are stains and blemishes.

Delighting in their mistakes when they feast on you. Having eyes full of adultery, and not ceasing to sin, luring unsteady souls, having the heart exercised in avarice, children of curse;

Who, leaving the right path, made a mistake following the path of Balaam, son of Beor, who loved the prize of injustice;

But he was rebuked for his transgression; the dumb donkey, speaking in a human voice, prevented the prophet's madness.

These are fountains without water, clouds carried by the force of the wind, for which the darkness of darkness eternally reserves itself.

Because, speaking very arrogant things about vanities, they are enticing with the lusts of the flesh, and with dissolutions, those who were turning away from those who walk in error.

Promising them freedom, being servants of corruption themselves. Because of whom someone is defeated, he is also made a servant. Because if, after having escaped the corruptions of the world, through the knowledge of the Lord and Savior Jesus Christ, they are again involved in them and overcome, their last state became worse than the first. For it would be better for them not to know the way of justice.

Than, knowing it, to deviate from the holy commandment that was given them. In this way, what happened by a true proverb says: The dog returned to its own vomit, and the sow was washed in the mud pits. **2 Peter 2: 1-22**

Jude reinforced Peter's words as to what would happen to Christians in the future, when apostasy spread throughout the land and the moral corruption of the church became a reality:

"For some have been introduced, who were already written for this same judgment, wicked men, who convert the grace of God into dissolution, and deny God, the only dominator and our Lord, Jesus Christ.

But I want to remind you, as to those who already knew this, that when the Lord saved a people, taking them out of the land of Egypt, he then destroyed those who did not believe;

And to the angels who did not keep their principality, but left their own habitation, he reserved in darkness and in eternal prisons until the judgment of that great day.

As well as Sodom and Gomorrah, and the surrounding cities, who, having given themselves up to fornication like those, and gone after another flesh, were put, for example, suffering the penalty of eternal fire.

And yet, these too, similarly asleep, contaminate their flesh, and reject domination, and vituperate dignities.

But the archangel Michael, when he contended with the devil, and disputed over the body of Moses, did not dare to pronounce a curse judgment against him; but he said, The Lord rebuke you.

These, however, speak ill of what they do not know; and, in what they naturally know, how irrational animals become corrupted. Woe to them! because they entered the path of Cain, and were taken in by the mistake of Balaam's prize, and perished in the contradiction of Korah.

These are stains in your feasts of love, feasting with you, and feeding themselves without fear; they are clouds without water, carried by winds from one place to another; they are like withered, fruitless trees, twice dead, uprooted.

Fiery waves of the sea, which skim their very abominations; wandering stars, for whom the blackness of darkness is forever reserved. And of these Enoch, the seventh after Adam, also prophesied, saying, Behold, the Lord is coming with thousands of his saints. To judge against all and to condemn all the wicked among them, for all their wicked works, which they wickedly committed.

And for all the harsh words that wicked sinners spoke against him.

These are mumblers, complainers of their luck, walking according to their lusts, and whose mouth says very arrogant things, admiring people because of interest.

But you, beloved, remember the words that were foretold to you by the apostles of our Lord Jesus Christ. Who told you that in recent times there would be scoffers who would walk according to their wicked lusts. These are the ones who separate themselves, sensual, who do not have the Spirit.

Judas 1: 4-19

For centuries the voice of Christ, apostles, prophets and the true church has echoed the world, warning about the danger of apostasy and separation between man and his Creator, because only when humanity understands that without God we can do nothing finally, so many plagues and epidemics will cease, the growth of violence, deaths, wars and all the misfortune that so destroys the hope of peace and happiness that we hope to one day achieve.

The Character of the Modern Christian

Nowadays it is no longer possible to identify with the naked eye the true Christians whose personalities are focused on the holiness required by God.

For true Christians (Heb 12:14), neither the same characteristics of the first disciples of Christ found in the early church, when the love of neighbor, the practice of mercy and sacrificial dedication to the Gospel were the greatest marks of those who identified themselves as children of the Most High (Acts 7: 54-60)

Religious modernism transformed all the religions of this present century into a real joke for skeptics who insist on the idea that there is no God and that Jesus Christ was just a lunatic, wanting to be recognized by humanity as being the Messiah awaited by Jews today.

Our religious leaders also lost their faith, followed after the apostasy of the last days and turned their ministries into a business where it became easy to earn money at the expense of the superstitions of others and the sale of gifts given to the church by the Holy Spirit so that they could carry out cures and miracles to convince sinners to repent.

As for the character of the Christian in recent times, what we can say is that the Christian church has never been so demoralized and without prestige, if centuries ago it was proud to identify itself as a believer in Jesus, today this causes embarrassment, because due to the large number of scandals caused by the brothers and the pastors who lead them.

Who should serve as a great example, the world began to see Christianity as a tremendous farce, a religious blow to enrich those who call themselves priests of the Most High God.

And the worst of all is that the unbelievers are right most of the time, because that is exactly what these mercenaries turned the Gospel and the church of Christ into, a true trade in indulgences in which only they get along.

Certainly one day, after death, everyone will be accountable for their actions before the great White Throne, but for the time being they still enjoy the juicy fruits of corruption and together with God's enemies they mock the sacrifice made by their Son on Calvary.

Corruption of Human Gender

Paul, Peter, Judas and many other church fathers warned about the bad times that would fall on the face of the earth, bringing all kinds of corruption to the human race. Christ himself warned us in the Gospels about the coming of false prophets, he described this crucial moment of humanity:

"And Jesus, answering, said to them: Beware that no one deceives you. For many will come in my name. Saying, I am the Christ, and they will deceive many.

And you will hear of wars and rumors of wars; look, do not be alarmed, because it must happen, but it is not yet the end.

For nation will rise against nation, and kingdom against kingdom, and there will be famines, and pests, and earthquakes, in various places. But all these things are the beginning of pain. Then they will give you up to be tormented, and they will kill you; and you will be hated by all nations because of my name.

In that time many will be scandalized, and will betray one another, and each other will hate each other. And many false prophets will arise, and they will deceive many. And as wickedness multiplies, the love of many will grow cold. But whoever endures to the end, he will be saved. Matthew 24: 4-13

Everything we are witnessing happen within the modern church and in society as a whole has been previously announced by the Lord. Nothing is new for those who truly gave their lives in the hands of the Master and listen to his voice that resonates in the pages of the Holy Bible, because in it we find the necessary revelations that keep us updated on everything that will happen in this world, both in the present and in the future. And as our eternal Master said, nothing that we contemplate today means that the end is near as many announce around in their alarming and pretentious preaching.

The corruption of mankind, wars, the increase in violence, the apostasy of faith and many other factors existing in the midst of this humanity that remains completely blind in spirit and alienated from God is only the "beginning of pains".

Dear reader, remember: We live in a world similar to Sodom and Gomorrah, just like the land of Canaan, when Joshua arrived there with God's people to take possession.

The inhabitants of that region lived in the practice of the worst types of sins, worshiped and gave their children to be burned alive as an offering to demons, they were considered abominable before the eyes of the Lord, they prostituted themselves, committed various types of crimes, they were disorderly and bloodthirsty. ..So we find ourselves today, surrounded by Canaanites and their insane acts. THEN TURN TO GOD!

As Características Morais da Verdadeira Igreja

Sometimes I come across some people who say they are interested in accepting Christ as the Savior of their souls but are in doubt as to which Christian church they should be a part of, they are aware that they need to surrender to the care of the Lord. They feel the need for that salvation in their hearts, their souls long for true deliverance from sin.

But the fear of choosing the wrong door to walk with Jesus and ending up with corrupt Christian groups prevents them from taking the first step. To these people doubtful about the sincerity of certain religious groups, I usually explain that it is impossible to identify a church or denomination where there are no scandals, feuds between the brothers, murmurings, disagreements and even a pastor who will use the money of the house of God for his own benefit. than they deserve as the scriptures recommend (1 Cor. 9:14)

However, we must look only at the true Christians and not at the tares - those false believers who will always dwell in the house of God in the midst of the wheat in order to cause scandals - because beforehand we were warned of the existence of these such by Jesus (Mt 13: 25.38.40) But it is possible to identify the true church of the Lord if we pay attention to its main moral characteristics, as these must reflect the personality of Christ, such as:

1. Holiness

2. Humility

3. Fervent Prayer

4. Total dedication to the cause of the Gospel

5. The ceaseless search for lost souls

6. Love God above all

7. Do not love money or accumulate material goods

8. Feeling like an outsider in this world

9. Wait for the rapture daily

10. Always remain faithful to the one who chose you as an elected nation

11. Never deny faith, even in the face of the worst suffering

12. Don't be ashamed of the cross of Christ

13. Live always willing to witness to the love of Christ and die for him if necessary.

The Character of Man as a Creature

There are different characteristics that differentiate man as a child or as a creature of God and the main one is voluntary sin. When we live alienated from our Creator, we feel pleasure in sinning and disgust everything that is directly linked to the divine and sacred.

As creatures we don't want to know rules, norms and we despise any and all warnings from the Spirit so that we can go back with our repeated rebellions.

The man separated from the love of God hates the light and loves the darkness, because the first reveals his infamous acts and the second covers his transgressions from the carnal eyes, from those who observe him in this world, however, in the eyes of the Almighty nothing is hidden and in the end you will have to account for all your iniquities, whether publicly or in secret.

While the first couple was in full communion with the Most High in Eden, there was joy in the friendship that united them, after the fall and the transgression they practiced, the bonds of affection were broken and since then humanity has been repulsed even to hear about God.

Jesus Christ, the Only Begotten, came to this world to change this depressing state in which the human soul is, but unfortunately not everyone is interested in remaking this communion. The character of man as a creature is shameful, depressing, morally poor and fallen, in need of an urgent change in his behavior so that after physical death his soul can once again enjoy the spiritual peace that only in God can we find.

The Character of Man as the Son of God

To be a son is to be an heir, deserving to receive part or all of the inheritance of a Father who longs to welcome all his children into his arms.

And protect them from any and all danger. Man as a son of God becomes his friend, is guided by his Spirit and no evil will touch him because he will send his angels to guard him in all his ways. David, a man after the Lord's heart, wrote:

"Because he will deliver you from the bird's snare, and from the pernicious plague. He will cover you with his feathers, and under his wings you will trust; your truth will be your shield and buckler. You will not be afraid of terror at night or the arrow that flies by day.

Not from the plague that walks in the dark, nor from the death toll that plagues at noon. A thousand will fall at your side, and ten thousand at your right, but it will not reach you.

Only with your eyes will you behold, and see the reward of the wicked.

For you, O Lord, are my refuge. In the Most High you made your dwelling. No harm will come to you, nor will any plague reach your tent. For he will give orders to your angels to guard you in all your ways.

They will hold you in their hands, lest you stumble with your foot in stone. You will tread on the lion and the snake; Thou shalt trample the lion and the serpent at his feet." **Psalm 91: 3-13**

When we are in complete harmony with the Father's will, he protects, keeps, listens and answers our prayers. About this, we read:

"And the Lord your God will make you prosper in all the work of your hands, in the fruit of your womb, and in the fruit of your animals, and in the fruit of your land for your good; because the Lord will rejoice in you to do you good, as he rejoiced in your fathers ". **Deuteronomy 30: 9**

"If you keep my commandments, you will remain in my love; just as I have kept my Father's commandments, and remain in his love. I have told you this, so that my joy may remain in you, and your joy may be complete. " **John 15: 10,11**

"And whatever we ask, we will receive from him, because we keep his commandments, and do what is pleasing to him. **1 John 3:22**

God's children eat from the best of their table, their prayers will be answered and their plans executed in the short term. Here is the reward of the righteous in this life.

General Considerations

The human character reflects the inner personality of each individual and is revealed externally through his actions and the moral conduct he exercises in the environment in which he lives. The different forms of character define who we are, both in the social, family, professional and in our deepest relationship with our Creator. People who tend to deny the existence of God are skeptical, empty, lackluster and generally unhappy. However, those who love him and give credit to his Word will prosper and reach the end of the celestial rainbow successfully.

Bibliography

Pentecostal Study Bible

New Life Bible

Wikipedia — Free Encyclopedia

Collaboration:

Pr. Antônio Carlos Magalhães Baía

Lightning Source UK Ltd.
Milton Keynes UK
UKRC012005270720
367275UK00005B/141